An Overview of the Endtime

Other Books by the Author

The Coming End of the Age

Preparing for the Lord's Return

The Goal and Peak of Our Christian Experience
Insights into Revelation, Book 1

The Beast, His Image, and His Mark
Insights into Revelation, Book 2

Firstfruits and Harvest
Insights into Revelation, Book 3

A Place Prepared
Insights into Revelation, Book 4

Delusion and God's Salvation

Greapa

The Coming of the King
in Matthew 24 and 25

Booklets by the Author

The Heart of God	Redemption and Salvation
The Heart of God II	Signs of the End
The Heart of God III	Urgency or Complacency
The Heart of God IV	A New Creation
The Heart of God V	The Spirit

Visit **aplaceinthewilderness.com** for more about these books (including their introduction, table of contents, and ordering information) and booklets.

An Overview of the Endtime

Paul Cozza

A Place in the Wilderness

An Overview of the Endtime

© 2024 Paul Cozza

ISBN 979-8-8693-8143-9

Paul Cozza
A Place in the Wilderness

Email: paul@aplaceinthewilderness.com
Website: aplaceinthewilderness.com

Scripture quotations are from the
American Standard Version of the Bible (1901)
unless otherwise noted.

Cover design: Nuggitz Creative Services (Nuggitz.com)
Cover Photo: Effi | iStockphoto.com

Table of Contents

Preface...1

Introduction 3

Chapter 1 – Signs of the End 5

The First Sign – Israel.....................................5

The Second Sign – Jerusalem 6

The Third Sign – The Falling Away 6

The Fourth Sign – Difficult Times..................7

The Fifth Sign – The Restraining One.............7

The Sixth Sign – Ten Nations..........................8

The Seventh Sign – The Antichrist..................8

The Eighth Sign – The Temple Mount Cleared 9

The Ninth Sign – The Pact................................9

Rebuilding the Temple....................................10

The Coming Empire 10

Chapter 2 – The Final Seven Years...............13

God's Dealings with Israel 13

The Covenant...14

Chapter 3 – God's Judgments.......................19

The First Four Seals 19

The Fifth Seal..20

The Sixth Seal...21

The Seventh Seal...22

The First Four Trumpets...................................22

The Fifth Trumpet 24

The Sixth Trumpet 25

The Seventh Trumpet 26

The First Five Bowls...27

The Sixth Bowl 29

The Seventh Bowl 30

Chapter 4 – The Church..**33**

The Great Reckoning 33

The Peak 34

The Time of Trouble 34

Caught Up 35

Chapter 5 – Israel **39**

The Covenant..39

The Final Years...39

Torment 40

The Final Battle 40

Chapter 6 – The Nations...**45**

Shock and Terror 45

Devastation...46

The End of the Nations 47

Chapter 7 – The Antichrist...**51**

The First Three and a Half Years...51

The Last Three and a Half Years 51

Chapter 8 – Ushering In the Kingdom **55**

Gathering Israel and the Nations 55

Face-to-face 56

Judgment 57

Establishing the Kingdom...58

Recovering the Earth 58

Chapter 9 – Conclusion **61**

Bibliography..**63**

Preface

Some years ago I wrote a detailed book[*] chronicling the events of the endtime. It touched upon all the endtime matters, putting them in chronological order. It incorporated copious footnotes, which explained many things not directly related to the text of the book. There were also numerous references.

However, because of its great detail, it is more of a reference work. I found that many who tried to read it were overwhelmed by the dense information within the book. It became clear that a simpler work about the endtime was necessary.

For this purpose, I have written this overview of the endtime. Although there are nine chapters in this book, most of them are quite short. The length of the book is also relatively brief. The content, although somewhat dense, should be straightforward and understandable.

I have endeavored to include only the most important events of the end. Consequently, certain significant happenings and individuals are omitted. For example, the ministries of Moses and Elijah and the works of the false prophet—the main ally of the Antichrist—are not covered. There are other matters that are also skipped. I have done this for simplicity.

I considered omitting references as well, but upon some reflection, I felt these are necessary. Many readers would desire to know the biblical source of what I have written.

I have also endeavored to keep explanatory footnotes to a minimum. Detailed explanations are often like going down the proverbial rabbit's hole. In an attempt to keep the text focused on the main items of the endtime, I have footnoted the text sparsely.

I hope the reader will find this book understandable and digestible. I also would point the reader to another book I have written, *Greapa*. All the main items of the endtime are incorporated into that fictional account; but while it is fiction, it is full

---

[*] *The Coming End of the Age*

of endtime biblical truths. It is certainly an easier and more enter-taining read than this somewhat dry overview.

There is one other matter of importance. As a kind of pre-requisite to this book, the reader should read the books of Daniel and Revelation at least one time. This will help immensely in understanding what is written in this book.

May the Lord bless every reader, not only with the know-ledge of the endtime, but with the hunger and thirst to gain Christ, to be prepared for what is coming upon the Earth.

Introduction

The endtime is very complex. There will be numerous momentous events taking place in a very brief time. Not only that, but God must also deal with three disparate peoples on the Earth: the Jews (Israel), the Christians (the Church), and the Gentiles (the nations). Each of these requires something particular from God to end the age. It is astounding that in only seven years, God can deal with everyone on the Earth and usher in Christ's kingdom.

To make the endtime less confusing, when we look at the final years of this age, we will look first at God's judgments during that time. We will then follow this by examining God's dealings during the endtime with each of the peoples on Earth separately. We will also look at the Antichrist during those final years as well.

We preface the endtime discussion with a chapter on the signs of the end. Knowing what must happen *before* the end will keep us from the euphoria or concern felt by many Christians due to the numerous false alarms that have happened and will happen, before the end is upon us.

Chapter 2 examines Daniel's prophecy in chapter 9 of his book. As we will see, this crucial portion of God's Word lays the foundation for all endtime prophecy.

In Chapter 3, God's endtime judgments are explored. Most of these judgments are seen in the seven seals, the seven trumpets, and the seven bowls.

Chapter 4 discusses the believers during the end. This portion passes from the rapture of the firstfruits, to the suffering of the majority of believers in the "wilderness" for three and a half years, to the harvesting of the remaining believers at the seventh trumpet.

Israel during the end is the subject of Chapter 5. In particular, her torment at the hands of the Antichrist during her great tribulation is examined.

Chapter 6 looks at the shock and terror that befalls the nations when God's judgments commence. It ends with Christ's destruction of all the armies of the nations who invade Israel as the age closes.

Chapter 7 traces the Antichrist and his movements from the time he first appears, until he is taken at Armageddon and judged.

In Chapter 8 we look at the happenings on Earth immediately after Israel is saved from destruction by Christ's appearing.

Chapter 9 is a short concluding word.

CHAPTER 1

Signs of the End

———————

What is meant by the terms "end" or "endtime?" By the "end," in a general sense, I mean the last few years of this age before the Lord's return. More specifically, I mean the last seven years of this age as prophesied by Daniel.[1]

Over the years, many have prophesied that the end was imminent, with some even declaring that certain events would happen on particular dates. Some have stated that the end was already upon us. All of these assertions have, of course, proven false.

Satan has, no doubt, been instigating such statements and using them for his purpose: the conditioning of humanity with many false prophecies to deceive mankind when the reality comes. These have led humanity to generally disregard warnings about the end. Like the boy who cried wolf, after many false declarations of woe, further declarations are dismissed as false.

However, with vision and understanding comes the assurance that certain events must happen before the end comes, because the Bible predicts them. At least nine great events must occur before or at the time of the end. Of these, two have happened, three are happening, and four are yet to come.

The First Sign – Israel

The first great sign was Israel becoming a nation. Israel must be a nation before the Lord returns, because when He does come back it will be to Israel[2] to save the Jewish people. Without the nation of Israel, the Lord cannot return.

After being dispersed and forsaken for millennia, somehow—by divine intervention—Israel came back into being in 1948. The three great earthly powers at that time—Great Britain, Russia, and the United States—in a mysterious confluence of interests, agreed to recognize and support the formation of the nation of Israel.

Although Israel was immediately attacked by the surrounding Arab nations, who sought to obliterate the fledgling nation, she survived and flourished. How could such a thing happen? It was because this was God's doing, and no power on Earth can undo what God does. This was the first clear sign of the Lord's second coming.

The Second Sign – Jerusalem

The second great sign was the return of Jerusalem into the hands of the Jews. In order for the end to come and the Lord to return, Jerusalem must be a part of Israel. Jerusalem will be given over to the nations for the last three and a half years of this age,[3] and so it must be in Israel's hands to be given over. Furthermore, when Christ returns, He will save Jerusalem from invading armies.[4]

This sign occurred in 1967. As Arabs massed to invade Israel, she preemptively struck, obliterating the forces poised to destroy her. In the process, Israel captured the Golan Heights from Syria, the Sinai from Egypt, and the west bank of the Jordan River from Jordan. Most importantly, Israel also took East Jerusalem from Jordan's control. What a great sign! Jerusalem was Israel's once again after about 1900 years.

At that time, the sense of the Lord's second coming was palpable to Christians. However, this was but the second of nine signs of His coming. His return was yet many years off: to us, a lifetime or more; to Him, but a brief hour or two.

The Third Sign – The Falling Away

Now we beseech you, brethren, touching the coming of our Lord Jesus Christ, and our gathering together unto him; to the end that ye be not quickly shaken from your mind, nor yet be troubled, either by spirit, or by word, or by epistle as from us, as that the day of the Lord is just at hand; let no man beguile you in any wise: for it will not be, except the falling away come first, and the man of sin be revealed, the son of perdition . . . (1 Thes. 2:1-3)

The next three signs are related, and are currently occurring. The first of these—the third great sign—is called the falling away.

The apostle Paul speaks of this falling away, or apostasy, from the faith in 1 Thessalonians.

Many who profess to be Christian actually are not. As the end nears, these are falling away from the faith. We can see this happening now. In many so-called Christian gatherings—gatherings that profess Christ—abominable things are allowed and even encouraged: homosexuality, abortion, politics, and the like. The Bible is often disregarded. Many leaders twist them to their benefit or to the benefit of the evil ideologies they follow. This will increase and get worse.

All of these are a fulfillment of the apostle Paul's word. It is by this that God is separating what is true from what is false, the wheat from the tares.[5]

The Fourth Sign – Difficult Times

But know this, that in the last days grievous times shall come. For men shall be lovers of self, lovers of money, boastful, haughty, railers, disobedient to parents, unthankful, unholy, without natural affection, implacable, slanderers, without self-control, fierce, no lovers of good, traitors, headstrong, puffed up, lovers of pleasure rather than lovers of God; holding a form of godliness, but having denied the power thereof: from these also turn away. (2 Tim. 2:1-5)

The fourth sign is mentioned by the apostle Paul in his second epistle to Timothy. All of what Paul declared there can now be plainly seen. The Earth is filled with evil and violence of all kinds. Politicians, business leaders, and much of the populace are not only evil, but boast and revel in that evil. They even attempt to force others to accept their evil and sinful ways. They are full of conceit and spite, and deny the Lord who created them.

The Fifth Sign – The Restraining One

And now ye know that which restraineth, to the end that he may be revealed in his own season. For the mystery of lawlessness doth already work: only there is one that restraineth now, until he be taken out of the way. (2 Thes. 2:6-7)

The fifth great sign is the removal of the restraining One. Throughout the centuries, evil has been restrained by the Spirit, who has limited evil, and kept it from advancing beyond a certain point. The tide of evil could only rise so high, and then was turned back. However, as the end approaches, the Spirit in His restraining power will withdraw, allowing evil a free course on Earth.

This will test the hearts of men: only men of good and godly heart will stand in the way as evil advances. In such circumstances, evil men, empowered by the evil one, will depart from the truth, as seen in the third sign. Men will be corrupted to the uttermost.

Even now, the restraining Spirit has withdrawn Himself—if not totally, then to a very great degree. The abundant, pervasive, and unchecked crime and violence we see today is a clear example of evil running rampant without restraint.

The Sixth Sign – Ten Nations

These next four signs—six through nine—are yet to come. The sixth sign is the formation of a ten-nation union or empire, which will arise around the Mediterranean. The Bible is clear: in various places[6] it prophesies of a ten-nation empire, over which the Antichrist will rule. It will be a latter-day Roman Empire centered around the Mediterranean and having Rome as its capital.

This has not yet occurred, but Great Britain leaving the European Union may be the start of the EU's demise. Eventually, many more nations will leave, including Italy and Greece. From all these nations around the Mediterranean, the ten-nation union will arise.

The Seventh Sign – The Antichrist

The seventh sign is the appearance of the Antichrist. Nearly all Christians are aware that in the endtime there will be one particularly evil person who is called the Antichrist.* He will arise from the midst of this ten-nation confederacy. At first, he will not

---

* In the Bible, he is called the beast, the little horn, and other names. Over the years he has come to be called the Antichrist.

be prominent, for he is called a *little* horn,[7] and not one of the ten leaders of the ten nations. In fact, it may not at first be in any way obvious that he is the coming Antichrist.

He must arise before the last seven years of this age because it is he who will sign the seven-year pact with Israel.[8] Therefore, he must have been around for some time in political circles before the end comes.

The Eighth Sign – The Temple Mount Cleared

The eighth sign is the removal of the Islamic religious structures currently occupying the Temple Mount—the Al-Aqsa Mosque and the Dome of the Rock. The Temple Mount is the site where the third Jewish Temple must be built. Consequently, it must be cleared. The darkness of Islam must be removed from the Temple Mount.

My understanding is that the Temple will be rebuilt on the site currently occupied by the Al-Aqsa Mosque. As a consequence, the mosque must be cleared away. I believe this will happen in the not-too-distant future.

Al-Aqsa will be razed and burnt to the ground. It will probably be destroyed from above in some unexpected way, for it is nearly impossible for this to occur by land because of the massive ground security surrounding that site.

The Ninth Sign – The Pact

The ninth and final sign will be the signing of the pact[9] between the Antichrist and Israel. This pact will mark the final seven years of this age for Israel and, in fact, for the whole Earth.

The pact will be between the Antichrist and Israel, and may include other nations as well, such as the Arab nations. When this pact comes into being, we will know that the end is at hand.

All of these signs must occur before the end. So, do not be shaken that the end is at hand, or misled that it is imminent. All these signs must happen first.

Rebuilding the Temple

You may wonder why I have omitted the rebuilding of the Temple as one of the great signs of the Lord's return. It is because I believe the Temple will be rebuilt during the beginning of those last seven years.

This is not obvious from scripture, but it seems to be implied. It is said of the last seven years that in the middle of them, the Antichrist will take away the sacrifice and oblation.[10] Why would this be mentioned in relation to the seven-year pact? It seems to imply that the pact must *allow* the sacrifice and oblation to begin.

However, before the Temple can be built, the altar must be set up and sacrifices offered to God. This was the order of things in Ezra's day.[11]

So then, if the pact allows the sacrifices and oblations to begin, it means that the altar with its sacrifices has not yet been set up. If that is the case, it then means that the Temple has not yet been built.

The Coming Empire

Based upon where we are now, the next great sign of the Lord's coming will be the formation of the ten-nation union arising from around the Mediterranean. While there may be many smaller indications of the Lord's return, this ten-nation union must come into being. Once it is exists, and the Antichrist has arisen from its midst, the end will likely come rapidly.

References

[1] Dan. 9:27

[2] For example, Zech. 12:1-9

[3] Rev. 11:2

[4] Zech. 12:1-5

[5] Matt. 13:30

[6] Dan. 7:7-8, 20-21, 24; Rev. 13:1, 17:3, 12

[7] Dan. 7:8; 8:9

[8] Dan. 9:27

[9] Dan. 9:27
[10] Dan. 9:27
[11] Ezra 3:2-6

CHAPTER 2

The Final Seven Years

———————

Although there is some debate in secular circles concerning the authority of the book of Daniel, according to the Lord Jesus, Daniel was real and a prophet, and his prophecies are true and shall be fulfilled.[1] Therefore, we can know assuredly what is written in the book of Daniel will come to pass.

God's Dealings with Israel

Seventy weeks are decreed upon thy people and upon thy holy city, to finish transgression, and to make an end of sins, and to make reconciliation for iniquity, and to bring in everlasting right-eousness, and to seal up vision and prophecy, and to anoint the most holy. Know therefore and discern, that from the going forth of the commandment to restore and to build Jerusalem unto the anointed one, the prince, shall be seven weeks, and threescore and two weeks: it shall be built again, with street and moat, even in troublous times. And after the threescore and two weeks shall the anointed one be cut off, and shall have nothing: and the people of the prince that shall come shall destroy the city and the sanctuary; and the end thereof shall be with a flood, and even unto the end shall be war; desolations are determined. And he shall make a firm covenant with many for one week: and in the midst of the week he shall cause the sacrifice and the oblation to cease; and upon the wing of abominations shall come one that maketh desolate; and even unto the full end, and that determined, shall wrath be poured out upon the desolate. (Dan. 9:24-27)

Daniel 9:24-27 is a crucial portion of God's Word. It presents the foundation upon which all endtime prophecies rest. These verses lay out the timeline of God's final dealings with the nation of Israel.

To understand this portion, we must first see that the Hebrew word* in these verses, often translated *weeks* or *week,* does not mean a period of seven days. Rather, this Hebrew word simply means a group of seven.

Here, Daniel is told seventy groups of seven, or 490, periods of time have been decreed upon Israel. The exact length of these time periods is not specified here, but from other portions in God's Word[2] we can determine that the period is 360 days. These are frequently called biblical or prophetic years. In the Bible, they are referred to as "times."[3] In one way or another, this period of 360 days occurs in a number of places in biblical prophecy.[4]

In this portion of Daniel, it says that there will be seventy periods of seven biblical years, or 490 years, during which six things are accomplished: finishing transgression, making an end of sins, making reconciliation for iniquity, bringing in everlasting righteousness, sealing up vision and prophecy, and anointing the Most Holy.

From the time the command went forth to rebuild Jerusalem until the time of Christ's death was 483 (69 groups of seven) prophetic years. This leaves one seven-year period that has yet to occur, during which God's dealings with Israel will be consummated. It is with this period of time, these last seven biblical years, that we are chiefly concerned. Most of what we cover in this book is concerned with those years.

The Covenant

This last group of seven years is sometimes referred to as Daniel's seventieth week. These final seven years of God's dealing with Israel are initiated by a firm covenant between the prince that will come (that is, the Antichrist) and Israel.

These verses in Daniel do not say what this covenant concerns, but it seems it will allow Israel to begin animal sacrifices again on the Temple Mount. In the middle of those final seven years, the Antichrist will break the covenant by causing the offerings at the Temple to cease, and then proceed to desolate Israel.

---

* shabua

There may be some kind of great turmoil in the Middle East in which Israel's existence will be threatened. Exactly what will happen, the Bible does not say. However, in the midst of that upheaval, the great leader of the ten-nation European empire will intervene to calm matters and bring about an apparent solution to all the Middle East problems. As mentioned above, he will make a pact with Israel and probably other nations as well.

While it would seem that peace had finally arrived in Israel, from the outset the great European leader (the Antichrist) will be deceiving everyone. The peace he offers, along with the other benefits of the covenant, will all be a charade. As we shall see, in the middle of that last week everything will change.

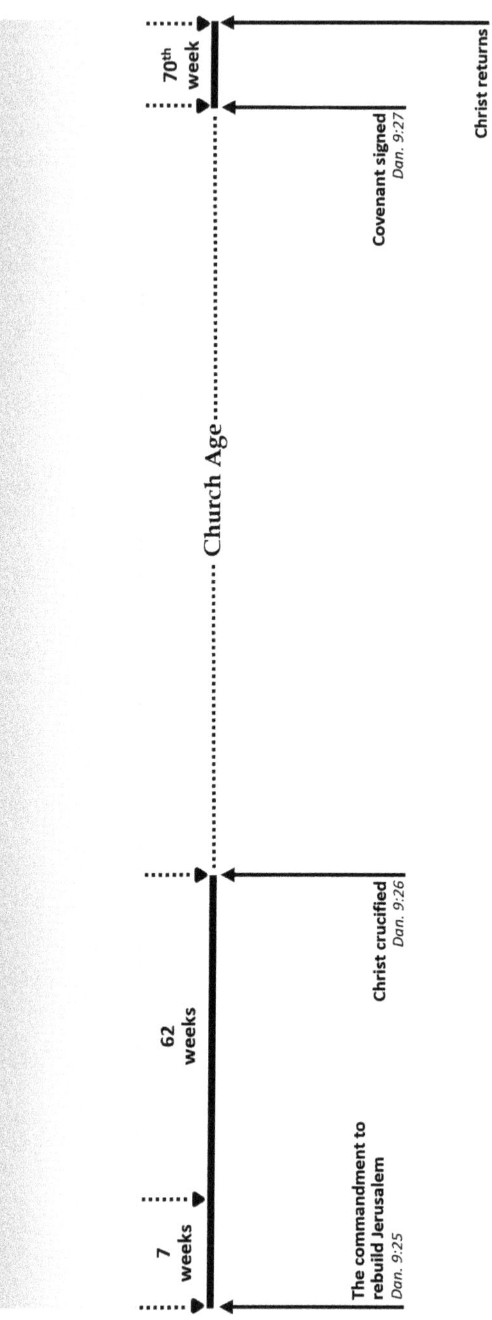

Daniel's Seventy Weeks
70th week
Church Age
Covenant signed
Dan. 9:27
Christ returns
Christ crucified
Dan. 9:26
62 weeks
7 weeks
The commandment to rebuild Jerusalem
Dan. 9:25

References

[1] Matt. 24:15

[2] E.g., Dan. 12:7; Rev. 12:6, 14

[3] Dan. 12:7; Rev. 12:14

[4] Dan. 9:24-27; 12:7; Rev. 11:2, 3; 12:6, 14; 13:5

CHAPTER 3

God's Judgments

———————————

Most of the endtime revolves around God's judgments. Through His many judgments, God ushers in Christ's kingdom on Earth, followed by the new heaven and new Earth with the New Jerusalem. The seven seals, seven trumpets, and seven bowls reveal most of God's judgments, especially of Israel and the nations. It is through these that God ends the godless evil of both mankind and Satan with his angels.

The First Four Seals

And I saw when the Lamb opened one of the seven seals, and I heard one of the four living creatures saying as with a voice of thunder, Come. And I saw, and behold, a white horse, and he that sat thereon had a bow; and there was given unto him a crown: and he came forth conquering, and to conquer. And when he opened the second seal, I heard the second living creature saying, Come. And another horse came forth, a red horse: and to him that sat thereon it was given to take peace from the earth, and that they should slay one another: and there was given unto him a great sword. And when he opened the third seal, I heard the third living creature saying, Come. And I saw, and behold, a black horse; and he that sat thereon had a balance in his hand. And I heard as it were a voice in the midst of the four living creatures saying, A measure of wheat for a shilling, and three measures of barley for a shilling; and the oil and the wine hurt thou not. And when he opened the fourth seal, I heard the voice of the fourth living creature saying, Come. And I saw, and behold, a pale horse: and he that sat upon him, his name was Death; and Hades followed with him. And there was given unto them authority over the fourth part of the earth, to kill with sword, and with famine, and with death, and by the wild beasts of the earth. (Rev. 6:1-8)

The seven seals disclose the happenings on Earth until the end of the age. The first four seals have been opened already. They depict the gospel, war, famine, and pestilence with death, all personified. These have been occurring from Christ's ascension, and will continue until the age closes. They correspond to what the Lord disclosed in Matthew 24.[1]

As the Lord sends forth the gospel into the whole Earth, Satan raises up war, famine, and pestilence with death, in an attempt to frustrate the gospel. Satan stirs up enmity between peoples and nations, thus causing wars. The wars result in food shortages and famines. The famines issue in disease and death. Yet, all of these simply help the gospel's progress. There is nothing the evil one can do to stop the gospel.

The Fifth Seal

And when he opened the fifth seal, I saw underneath the altar the souls of them that had been slain for the word of God, and for the testimony which they held: and they cried with a great voice, saying, How long, O Master, the holy and true, dost thou not judge and avenge our blood on them that dwell on the earth? And there was given them to each one a white robe; and it was said unto them, that they should rest yet for a little time, until their fellow-servants also and their brethren, who should be killed even as they were, should have fulfilled their course. (Rev. 6:9-11)

The result of all this conflict between the gospel of Christ and what He has done, and Satan's efforts to overcome the gospel, is the slaughter of many Christians. When Satan realizes his attempts are futile, he resorts to murder to try to stop God's move through the gospel. How many Christian saints he has martyred over the centuries, only God knows.

These martyrs are seen when the fifth seal is opened. They are depicted under the earth, awaiting God's judgment of godless mankind. They are crying out for God's vengeance as their number increases dramatically by the intense persecution of the endtime. The martyrs are told to wait a short while, and are given white robes—apparel of approval, in which they can stand before God on the throne after their imminent resurrection.

The Sixth Seal

And I saw when he opened the sixth seal, and there was a great earthquake; and the sun became black as sackcloth of hair, and the whole moon became as blood; and the stars of the heaven fell unto the earth, as a fig tree casteth her unripe figs when she is shaken of a great wind. And the heaven was removed as a scroll when it is rolled up; and every mountain and island were moved out of their places. And the kings of the earth, and the princes, and the chief captains, and the rich, and the strong, and every bond-man and freeman, hid themselves in the caves and in the rocks of the mountains; and they say to the mountains and to the rocks, Fall on us, and hide us from the face of him that sitteth on the throne, and from the wrath of the Lamb: for the great day of their wrath is come; and who is able to stand? (Rev. 6:12-17)

And I will show wonders in the heavens and in the earth: blood, and fire, and pillars of smoke. The sun shall be turned into darkness, and the moon into blood, before the great and terrible day of Jehovah cometh. (Joel 2:30-31)

The sixth seal reveals God's response to the cry of the martyrs from under the earth. A massive earthquake shakes the Earth, the sun is blackened, and the moon turns blood-red. Stars fall from heaven like a fig tree losing its unripe figs in a great wind.

The "stars" falling from heaven are a massive swarm of asteroids and meteors passing through the Earth's atmosphere. Many of these will strike the Earth, producing great pillars of smoke. The enormous amount of debris spewed into the air, coupled with the atmospheric remnants of the numerous burning meteors and asteroids, in turn, will darken the sun. On the opposite side of the sky, where the haze in the atmosphere will be less, it will cause the moon to turn red. A gigantic earthquake will result from the many impacts of large asteroids.

These are all a warning to those dwelling on the Earth of what is about to occur. The events of the sixth seal are a foretaste of what will happen when the seventh seal is opened and the first four trumpets sound. Realizing God's impending judgment, men of all sorts will seek to hide themselves under the earth from the great destruction that will shortly occur. The opening of this seal is the start of what the Bible calls *the time of trial,* which is about to come upon the whole inhabited Earth.[2]

The Seventh Seal

And when he opened the seventh seal, there followed a silence in heaven about the space of half an hour. And I saw the seven angels that stand before God; and there were given unto them seven trumpets. And another angel came and stood over the altar, having a golden censer; and there was given unto him much incense, that he should add it unto the prayers of all the saints upon the golden altar which was before the throne. And the smoke of the incense, with the prayers of the saints, went up before God out of the angel's hand. And the angel taketh the censer; and he filled it with the fire of the altar, and cast it upon the earth: and there followed thunders, and voices, and lightnings, and an earthquake. And the seven angels that had the seven trumpets prepared themselves to sound. (Rev. 8:1-6)

When Christ opens the seventh seal, there is silence in heaven for about half an hour. This indicates the great seriousness of God's impending judgments.

Christ—depicted as "another angel"*—then offers to God incense with the prayers of the saints, those believers who are left on the Earth to pass through this extraordinary time. They are no doubt praying both for God's judgment and for His protection during the cataclysms about to strike the Earth.

Christ takes fire from the altar and casts it to the Earth. This fire should be numerous asteroids and meteors striking the Earth. It is accompanied by another great earthquake. This will be the beginning of the troubles of the last three and a half years. As seen in these verses, this seal also includes the seven trumpets.

The First Four Trumpets

And the seven angels that had the seven trumpets prepared themselves to sound. And the first sounded, and there followed

---

* Christ is depicted as "another angel" four times in the book of Revelation, in verse 7:2, 8:3, 10:1, and 18:1.

hail and fire, mingled with blood, and they were cast upon the earth: and the third part of the earth was burnt up, and the third part of the trees was burnt up, and all green grass was burnt up. And the second angel sounded, and as it were a great mountain burning with fire was cast into the sea: and the third part of the sea became blood; and there died the third part of the creatures which were in the sea, even they that had life; and the third part of the ships was destroyed. And the third angel sounded, and there fell from heaven a great star, burning as a torch, and it fell upon the third part of the rivers, and upon the fountains of the waters; and the name of the star is called Wormwood: and the third part of the waters became wormwood; and many men died of the waters, because they were made bitter. And the fourth angel sounded, and the third part of the sun was smitten, and the third part of the moon, and the third part of the stars; that the third part of them should be darkened, and the day should not shine for the third part of it, and the night in like manner. (Rev. 8:6-12)

The seven trumpets show us God's particular judgments on the most evil of those dwelling on Earth. The first four of these trumpets are judgments upon the land, the sea, the rivers and fountains of waters, and the sky, respectively. These, along with the sixth and seventh seals, are different aspects of one great and momentous event.

The sixth seal depicts numerous meteors and asteroids passing through Earth's atmosphere and, according to Joel,[3] a number of them striking Earth. These are a precursor to what is seen when the seventh seal is opened and the first four trumpets sound. At that time, an enormous swarm of asteroids of various sizes will strike the Earth, causing unspeakable destruction. A pair of these asteroids will be colossal, with one—seen in the second trumpet—apparently measuring miles in diameter.

In the first four trumpets God will judge Asia,* the Pacific and Pacific Rim,† the Himalayas and the water flowing from there

---

* Only Asia is large enough to account for "the third of the earth."

† Only Pacific is large enough to account for "the third of the sea."

to Asia,* and the sky above these areas. Vast areas of the Earth will be obliterated. Other areas will be devastated by fires and incredible winds. Towering tsunamis will destroy coastlines. Erupting volcanoes will produce great rivers of lava and spew massive clouds of ash into the atmosphere. The Earth, as we now know it, will simply cease to be. However, for the sake of Israel, southern Europe and the Middle East will largely be spared these judgments.

The Fifth Trumpet

And the fifth angel sounded, and I saw a star from heaven fallen unto the earth: and there was given to him the key of the pit of the abyss. And he opened the pit of the abyss; and there went up a smoke out of the pit, as the smoke of a great furnace; and the sun and the air were darkened by reason of the smoke of the pit. And out of the smoke came forth locusts upon the earth; and power was given them, as the scorpions of the earth have power. And it was said unto them that they should not hurt the grass of the earth, neither any green thing, neither any tree, but only such men as have not the seal of God on their foreheads. And it was given them that they should not kill them, but that they should be tormented five months: and their torment was as the torment of a scorpion, when it striketh a man. And in those days men shall seek death, and shall in no wise find it; and they shall desire to die, and death fleeth from them. And the shapes of the locusts were like unto horses prepared for war; and upon their heads as it were crowns like unto gold, and their faces were as men's faces. And they had hair as the hair of women, and their teeth were as the teeth of lions. And they had breastplates, as it were breastplates of iron; and the sound of their wings was as the sound of chariots, of many horses rushing to war. And they have tails like unto scorpions, and stings; and in their tails is their power to hurt men five months. (Rev. 9:1-10)

The fifth trumpet will occur sometime after the first four trumpets. How long a time is unknown. When the fifth trumpet

---

* Only the rivers and waters flowing from the Himalayas can account for "the third of the waters."

sounds, demons rising from the shaft of the abyss will possess the Antichrist's army.* They will then torment Israel† with some sort of device the causes excruciating pain. That agony will be so intense that men will seek to die, yet death will escape them. This anguish will continue for five grueling months.

This suffering will begin to soften the hardened hearts of unbelieving Israel. For so long, the Jews have rejected and hated Jesus, although He came to die for them. This judgment from God will be one of the agonies Israel will pass through to prepare them for the coming of their Messiah.

The Sixth Trumpet

And the sixth angel sounded, and I heard a voice from the horns of the golden altar which is before God, one saying to the sixth angel that had the trumpet, Loose the four angels that are bound at the great river Euphrates. And the four angels were loosed, that had been prepared for the hour and day and month and year, that they should kill the third part of men. And the number of the armies of the horsemen was twice ten thousand times ten thousand: I heard the number of them. And thus I saw the horses in the vision, and them that sat on them, having breastplates as of fire and of hyacinth and of brimstone: and the heads of the horses are as the heads of lions; and out of their mouths proceedeth fire and smoke and brimstone. By these three plagues was the third part of men killed, by the fire and the smoke and the brimstone, which proceeded out of their mouths. For the power of the horses is in their mouth, and in their tails: for their tails are like unto serpents, and have heads; and with them they hurt. And the rest of mankind, who were not killed with these plagues, repented not of the works of their hands, that they should not worship demons, and the idols of gold, and of silver, and of brass, and of stone, and of wood; which can neither see, nor hear, nor walk: and they

---

* While the locusts ascending from the shaft of the abyss are demons, the depiction of them in these verses is of men. Therefore, this indicates the men—the Antichrist's army—are demon-possessed.

† The fact that the sealed (of Israel) escape this torment indicates that this suffering is directed toward Israel.

repented not of their murders, nor of their sorceries, nor of their fornication, nor of their thefts. (Rev. 9:13-21)

The sixth trumpet unveils God's further judgment of Asia.[*] Two hundred million "horsemen" will advance across Asia, murdering as they go. This will continue for an hour, plus a day, plus a month, plus a year—13 months plus 25 hours. In the process, they will kill a third of mankind. The slaughter will be unspeakable.

When describing these armies, John must have seen modern-day vehicles and weapons. The horses have heads like lions—that is, they have grills like the vehicles of today's militaries. The fire, smoke, and brimstone—proceeding out of the mouths of these horses—should depict the gun and rifle fire, along with missiles and rockets, of modern armies. The tails should refer to the artillery pieces or other weapons being drawn behind military vehicles.

In his description, John had to use the terminology of his time. He did not have words such as tanks, Jeeps, troop carriers, rocket launchers, or fuel trucks. I believe what he saw, sweeping across the Asian continent, were a number of great armies, comprised of vehicles of many sorts, armed combatants mounted on literal horses, and hordes of foot soldiers.

After the judgments of the first four trumpets, much of the Asian mainland will have been decimated. What remains of the militaries—armed forces that will have been sheltered underground to somehow protect them from that great destruction—will come forth. After stripping the land of every remaining resource, they will begin their march toward the Middle East, massacring everyone in their path.

This will be yet another judgment upon a godless Asia, one that had martyred so many Christians. Even under so much distress, the ones who escape this slaughter will still not repent.

The Seventh Trumpet

And the seventh angel sounded; and there followed great voices in heaven, and they said, The kingdom of the world is become the

---

[*] What other area could field an army of 200,000,000!

kingdom of our Lord, and of his Christ: and he shall reign for ever and ever. And the four and twenty elders, who sit before God on their thrones, fell upon their faces and worshipped God, saying, We give thee thanks, O Lord God, the Almighty, who art and who wast; because thou hast taken thy great power, and didst reign. And the nations were wroth, and thy wrath came, and the time of the dead to be judged, and the time to give their reward to thy servants the prophets, and to the saints, and to them that fear thy name, the small and the great; and to destroy them that destroy the earth. And there was opened the temple of God that is in heaven; and there was seen in his temple the ark of his covenant; and there followed lightnings, and voices, and thunders, and an earthquake, and great hail. (Rev. 11:15-19)

The seventh trumpet occurs at the very end of the age. It is God's final judgment of the age. This trumpet includes the descent of Christ to the air,[4] the resurrection of the dead saints,[5] the catching up to the air of both the resurrected saints and those saints who are living and remain on Earth,[6] the judgment seat of Christ,[7] the reward to the worthy saints, the descent of Christ to the Earth,[8] the destruction of all the armies invading Israel, the capture and judgment of the Antichrist,[9] and the judgment of the nations at the valley of Jehoshaphat.[10] It also includes the seven bowls.[11]

The First Five Bowls

And I heard a great voice out of the temple, saying to the seven angels, Go ye, and pour out the seven bowls of the wrath of God into the earth. And the first went, and poured out his bowl into the earth; and it became a noisome and grievous sore upon the men that had the mark of the beast, and that worshipped his image. And the second poured out his bowl into the sea; and it became blood as of a dead man; and every living soul died, even the things that were in the sea. And the third poured out his bowl into the rivers and the fountains of the waters; and it became blood. And I heard the angel of the waters saying, Righteous art thou, who art and who wast, thou Holy One, because thou didst thus judge: for they poured out the blood of saints and prophets, and blood hast thou given them to drink: they are worthy. And I heard the altar saying, Yea, O Lord God, the Almighty, true and righteous are thy judgments. And the fourth poured out his bowl upon the sun; and it was given unto it to scorch men with fire. And men were scorched with great heat: and they blasphemed the name of God who hath the power over these plagues; and they repented not to give him glory. And the fifth poured out his bowl upon the throne of the beast; and his kingdom was darkened; and they gnawed their tongues for pain, and they blasphemed the God of heaven because of their pains and their sores; and they repented not of their works. (Rev. 16:1-10)

The seven bowls end God's judgments; they finish God's wrath upon godless humanity.[12] As mentioned in the description of the seventh trumpet[13] all these plagues will occur in a very short time, a matter of only a few days.

The first five bowls are upon the land, the sea, the rivers and fountains of waters, the sun, and the throne of the Antichrist and his empire respectively. As indicated in the first and fifth bowl, these judgments are particularly upon the Antichrist and his empire. That area, which was largely spared the judgments of the first four trumpets, will face the most severe outpouring of God's wrath at the very end of the age.

The first five bowls may be different aspects of one great event, similar to the first four trumpets. In the first bowl, something from the earth infects those who have the mark of the beast.* The result is an offensive and painful sore, probably at the very site of that mark.

In the second bowl, the sea—that is, the Mediterranean Sea—becomes like the congealed blood of a dead man. Who can say what would cause the sea to change in such a way.

In the third bowl, the rivers and fountains of waters became blood. These rivers and fountains should be those flowing from the Alps, and this judgment should be upon those peaks. In some way, the rivers and fountains of waters in these mountains will be turned into something seen as blood. This may be a reflection of the searing heat seen in the fourth bowl.

The fourth bowl will be poured out upon the sun, and the sun will scorch men with great heat. Something will happen in the

---

* The mark of the beast is his name or the number of his name imprinted or implanted upon the right hand or forehead of his followers.

sun to cause it to eject great sun flares, which will, in turn, burn those in Antichrist's empire. The timing of these events is extraordinary. The flares will shoot forth from the sun at just the right moment to burn only those of the Antichrist's empire, as the Earth turns on its axis.

The fifth bowl will be poured out upon the throne of the beast. That is, it will be poured out upon Rome. Somehow, this will cause great darkness upon the Antichrist's kingdom. This will not be ordinary darkness, but one that in some way causes great pain.

In all these judgments, God is seeking to bring men to repentance, but they will not repent.

The Sixth Bowl

And the sixth poured out his bowl upon the great river, the river Euphrates; and the water thereof was dried up, that the way might be made ready for the kings that come from the sunrising. And I saw coming out of the mouth of the dragon, and out of the mouth of the beast, and out of the mouth of the false prophet, three unclean spirits, as it were frogs: for they are spirits of demons, working signs; which go forth unto the kings of the whole world, to gather them together unto the war of the great day of God, the Almighty. (Behold, I come as a thief. Blessed is he that watcheth, and keepeth his garments, lest he walk naked, and they see his shame.) And they gathered them together into the place which is called in Hebrew Har-Magedon. (Rev. 16:12-16)

The sixth bowl will be poured out upon the river Euphrates. That great river will be dried up, allowing the hosts sweeping toward Israel to pass over it. The kings from the sunrising (i.e., from the east) will be the leaders of the great Asian hordes, which will advance toward Israel.

As indicated by the wording here, this bowl includes the battle at Armageddon. Demons will come forth from the mouths of Satan, the Antichrist, and his compatriot (the "false prophet"), to gather all the armies coming upon Israel to that great battle at Armageddon.

Pay close attention to verse 15 in this passage. Even by the time the demons go forth to draw Earth's armies to Armageddon, there will be believers on Earth, whom the Lord warns about His coming.

The Seventh Bowl

And the seventh poured out his bowl upon the air; and there came forth a great voice out of the temple, from the throne, saying, It is done: and there were lightnings, and voices, and thunders; and there was a great earthquake, such as was not since there were men upon the earth, so great an earthquake, so mighty. And the great city was divided into three parts, and the cities of the nations fell: and Babylon the great was remembered in the sight of God, to give unto her the cup of the wine of the fierceness of his wrath. And every island fled away, and the mountains were not found. And great hail, every stone about the weight of a talent, cometh down out of heaven upon men: and men blasphemed God because of the plague of the hail; for the plague thereof is exceeding great. (Rev. 16:17-21)

The seventh bowl includes an incredibly massive earthquake, the likes of which has never been experienced by man. It is accompanied by hail weighing about 100 pounds (about 45 kilograms). This all seems to occur as Christ is slaughtering His enemies in Israel.

The massive earthquake may strike as Christ is setting His feet down on the Mount of Olives, splitting it in half. The great hail may fall particularly upon the armies gathered against Christ in Israel.

Rome (Babylon the great) will be destroyed; Jerusalem will be divided into three parts; all the islands will disappear, and the mountains will no longer be found. How great this earthquake will be!

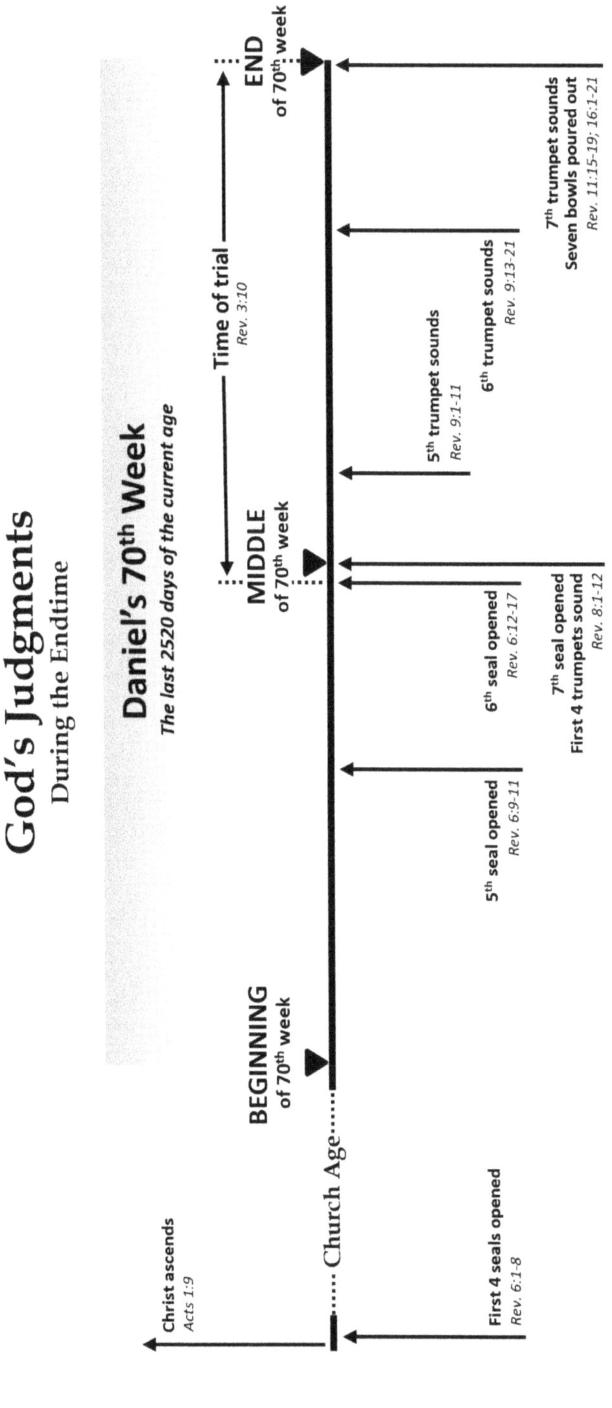
God's Judgments
During the Endtime
Daniel's 70th Week
The last 2520 days of the current age
Time of trial
Rev. 3:10
Christ ascends
Acts 1:9
Church Age
BEGINNING
of 70th week
MIDDLE
of 70th week
END
of 70th week
First 4 seals opened
Rev. 6:1-8
5th seal opened
Rev. 6:9-11
6th seal opened
Rev. 6:12-17
7th seal opened
First 4 trumpets sound
Rev. 8:1-12
5th trumpet sounds
Rev. 9:1-11
6th trumpet sounds
Rev. 9:13-21
7th trumpet sounds
Seven bowls poured out
Rev. 11:15-19; 16:1-21

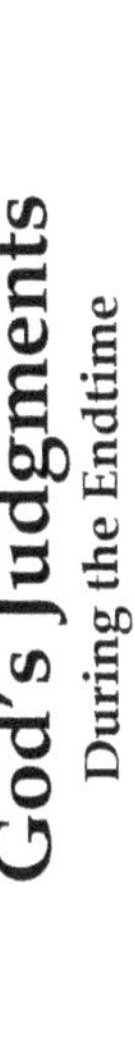

References

[1] Matt. 24:4-14

[2] Rev. 3:10

[3] Joel 2:30

[4] 1 Thes. 4:16; 1 Cor. 15:52

[5] 1 Thes. 4:16

[6] 1 Thes. 4:17

[7] 2 Cor. 5:10

[8] Rev. 19:11-15

[9] Rev. 19:19-20

[10] Joel 3:1-2; Matt. 25:31-46

[11] Cf. Rev. 11:19 and Rev. 16:18, 21

[12] Rev. 15:1

[13] Rev. 10:7

CHAPTER 4

The Church

As we will see, the endtime for Christians is, in some sense, the simplest of the three peoples on Earth. However, because it is the simplest does not mean it is simple.

As the final three and a half years of this age approach, Christians will be persecuted intensely and suffering greatly. It appears such persecution may have already begun.

The Great Reckoning

In the midst of this persecution, a moment of great reckoning will come upon all Christians. The troubles that will strike the Earth are not actually for Christians, but for Israel and the world. It is God's desire every Christian would be mature and taken from the Earth when that moment of reckoning comes. Unfortunately, many—perhaps even most—Christians will not be properly prepared to be taken to stand before the Lord and escape those troubles.[1]

Therefore, when that instant comes, only some will be taken and the rest will be left.* When that will take place, no one knows except the Father. As mentioned in Luke 21, it must occur before the great upheavals of the sixth and seventh seals and first four trumpets. However, whether it occurs before the final seven years, or sometime during the beginning of those years, no one can say. We must be ready at all times, for the Lord will come *as a thief.* Consequently, the Lord tells us to watch and to be ready.[2]

---

* See *The Coming End of the Age*, Chapter 3, or *Firstfruits and Harvest* for a detailed discussion of this controversial matter.

The Peak

The ones who have matured and been perfected will be taken to stand with the Lord Jesus before the Father.[3] There, they will celebrate the coming of God's kingdom and God's marvelous salvation, which brought them from what they once were to the highest state there is or can be. It is this goal that we all must seek. This is the peak of our Christian experience. There has never been, nor will there ever be again, such an experience! For eternity, those who are accounted worthy to stand before the Lord in that day will recall the ecstasy of that celebration when they sang hymns to the dear Father and savored the sweetness of all that He is and has done.

The Time of Trouble

And the woman fled into the wilderness, where she hath a place prepared of God, that there they may nourish her a thousand two hundred and threescore days. (Rev. 12:6)

Those Christians who are left behind on the Earth will pass through the tumultuous events of the endtime—something the Bible calls the time of trouble.[4] They will flee to a place prepared by God in the wilderness, where they will be nourished for three and a half years. They need to be *nourished* because they are spiritually undernourished, and it is for this reason that they never grew to maturity. These Christians lacked the proper spiritual food by which they could mature in Christ.

Those three and a half years will be extraordinarily hard. Christians will be struggling to survive—to eat, drink, and even breathe. The whole order of things on Earth will have been destroyed. There will be nothing left of the world they once knew and loved.

In such an environment and predicament, all the doctrines and practices that have divided the Christians will be dropped. It may take some time for this to occur, but in the intense pressure of those last three and a half years, those trivial divisive things will be discarded and disappear. Most of the Christians will come back to Christ, and Christ alone. It is Him upon whom they should have been focusing their entire lives.

Caught Up

For this we say unto you by the word of the Lord, that we that are alive, that are left unto the coming of the Lord, shall in no wise precede them that are fallen asleep. For the Lord himself shall descend from heaven, with a shout, with the voice of the archangel, and with the trump of God: and the dead in Christ shall rise first; then we that are alive, that are left, shall together with them be caught up in the clouds, to meet the Lord in the air: and so shall we ever be with the Lord. (1 Thes. 4:15-17)

Near the end of those last three and a half years, the seventh trumpet will sound. By then, the Christians will have been dried out of all the worldly water,[5] which they had previously enjoyed and had partaken of freely. But even by that time, some living believers will still not be ready.[6]

The dead in Christ will be resurrected. They will be caught up with the living believers to meet Christ in the air. There, all the believers will stand before the judgment seat of Christ and give an account for the things they did in the body, whether good or bad.[7]

Some will be judged worthy of reward and enter into the joy of the Lord during the Millennium.[8] The remainder will suffer discipline during those thousand years.[9]

Christ will then marry His bride—an eternal marriage.[10] He, with his bride and all his redeemed, along with His angels, will then descend to destroy those who are destroying Israel.[11]

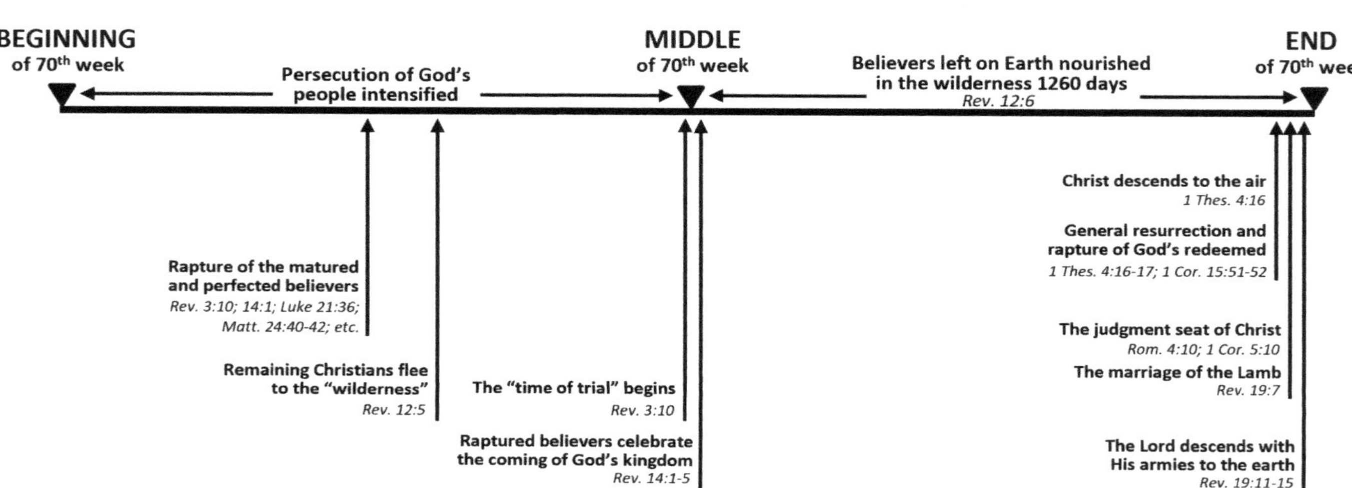

The Church
During the Endtime
Daniel's 70th Week
The last 2520 days of the current age
BEGINNING
of 70th week
MIDDLE
of 70th week
END
of 70th week
Persecution of God's people intensified
Believers left on Earth nourished in the wilderness 1260 days
Rev. 12:6
Christ descends to the air
1 Thes. 4:16
General resurrection and rapture of God's redeemed
1 Thes. 4:16-17; 1 Cor. 15:51-52
The judgment seat of Christ
Rom. 4:10; 1 Cor. 5:10
The marriage of the Lamb
Rev. 19:7
The Lord descends with His armies to the earth
Rev. 19:11-15
Rapture of the matured and perfected believers
Rev. 3:10; 14:1; Luke 21:36; Matt. 24:40-42; etc.
Remaining Christians flee to the "wilderness"
Rev. 12:5
The "time of trial" begins
Rev. 3:10
Raptured believers celebrate the coming of God's kingdom
Rev. 14:1-5

References

[1] Luke 21:36
[2] Matt. 24:42, 44
[3] Rev. 14:1-5
[4] Rev. 3:10
[5] Rev. 14:15 (Greek)
[6] Rev. 16:15
[7] 2 Cor. 5:10
[8] Matt. 25:21, 23
[9] Matt. 25:6-12
[10] Rev. 19:7
[11] Rev. 19:11-14

CHAPTER 4

Israel

____

The situation in Israel during the endtime is quite complicated. This is both understandable and needed, given the great hatred within the Jews toward Christ. To break through that delusional hatred, extraordinary measures are necessary.

The Covenant

And he shall make a firm covenant with many for one week: and in the midst of the week he shall cause the sacrifice and the oblation to cease . . . (Dan. 9:27)

At the end of this age, the Antichrist will make a firm covenant with the Jews. This will last for seven (biblical) years, or 2520 days. This pact will probably come about as a result of some serious, existential crisis to Israel. Although we are not told the terms of that covenant, it appears that it will include the provision that Israel can once again offer animal sacrifices.

During the first half of those last seven years, Israel will become extremely prosperous[1] and rejoice in their supposed security.[2] They, like the nations, will not suspect what is about to happen. But many in Israel will prophesy, dream dreams, and see visions[3]—dreams and visions, no doubt, about endtime happenings.

The Final Years

Suddenly[4] everything will change, with a number of momentous events occurring within a very short time:

- The signs recorded in Joel 2 will occur: pillars of smoke, the sun darkened, and the moon turned to blood-red.[5]

- Then, 144,000 Jews will be sealed.[6] These are most likely those who received the visions, dreamed the dreams, and prophesied. All those extraordinary happenings will be preparing them to believe in and receive Christ, when the events—which they saw in visions and dreams—come to pass.

- The Antichrist will cause the animal sacrifices to cease.[7] He will then sit in the temple, claiming to be God.[8]

The whole Earth will be in upheaval due to the events of the sixth and seventh seals and the first four trumpets, all of which will occur about this same time. There will then be a period of unknown duration before Israel's intense suffering begins.[9]

Torment

When the fifth trumpet sounds, the Antichrist's demon-possessed army will begin tormenting the Jews.[10] This will be the start of the great tribulation to Israel.[11]

An image of the Antichrist—an idol that talks—will be set up in the Temple.[12] Jerusalem will be surrounded by the Antichrist's forces.[13] Hearing of these events, the 144,000 who had been sealed will flee to the mountains.[14] Then the unspeakable torment will commence. Men will seek to die but be unable to do so.[15] This will continue for five months.[16]

The Final Battle

Torments of one form or another will continue in Israel until right before the end of the age.[17] Then, three great armies will gather in Israel for a final battle against one another.[18] Despairing of their own existence, the despondent Jews will then see the sign of the Son of Man appear in the heavens,[19] leading all of Israel to finally repent to the Lord.[20]

The heavens will then part, and Christ will appear[21] to deliver Israel from the invading armies. He will descend to slaughter all of these forces, starting from Bozrah.[22] His feet will stand on the Mount of Olives,[23] cleaving it from East to West. The inhabitants of Jerusalem will flee into the cleft of the Mount.[24] Christ will then destroy the nearby armies with the brightness of His appearing.[25] This great battle will end at Armageddon.[26] There, the Antichrist will be taken and cast into the lake of fire.[27]

The great tribulation will be over and all Israel will be saved.[28]

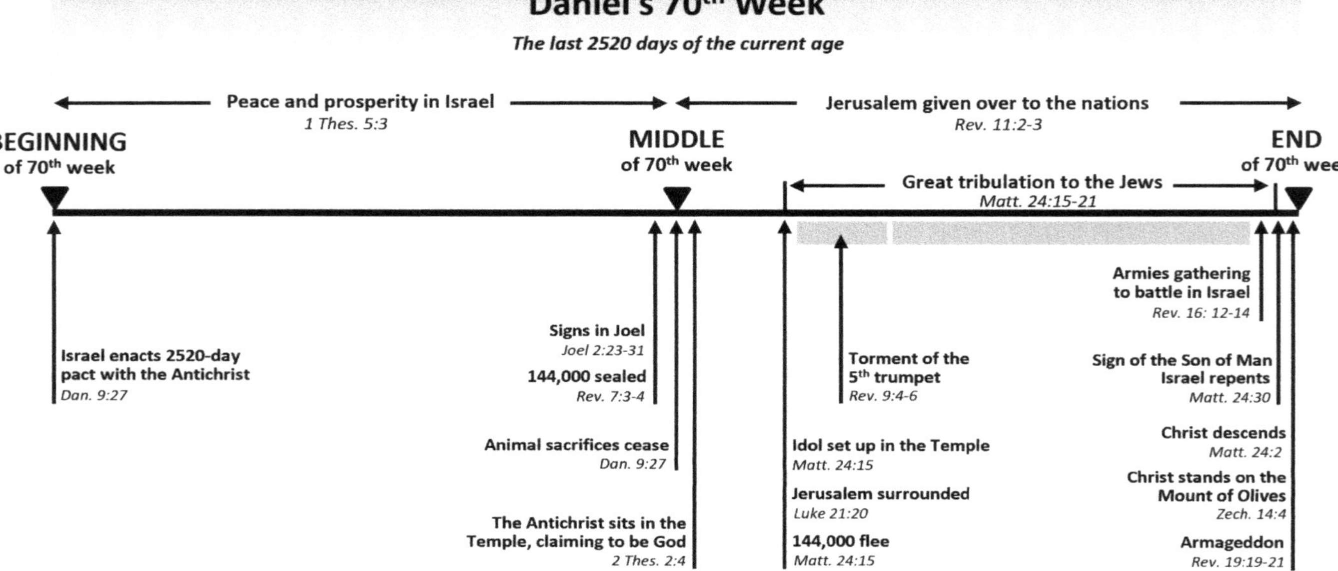

Israel
During the Endtime

Daniel's 70th Week
The last 2520 days of the current age

Peace and prosperity in Israel
1 Thes. 5:3

Jerusalem given over to the nations
Rev. 11:2-3

BEGINNING
of 70th week

MIDDLE
of 70th week

END
of 70th week

Great tribulation to the Jews
Matt. 24:15-21

Israel enacts 2520-day
pact with the Antichrist
Dan. 9:27

Signs in Joel
Joel 2:23-31

144,000 sealed
Rev. 7:3-4

Animal sacrifices cease
Dan. 9:27

The Antichrist sits in the
Temple, claiming to be God
2 Thes. 2:4

Torment of the
5th trumpet
Rev. 9:4-6

Idol set up in the Temple
Matt. 24:15

Jerusalem surrounded
Luke 21:20

144,000 flee
Matt. 24:15

Armies gathering
to battle in Israel
Rev. 16: 12-14

Sign of the Son of Man
Israel repents
Matt. 24:30

Christ descends
Matt. 24:2

Christ stands on the
Mount of Olives
Zech. 14:4

Armageddon
Rev. 19:19-21

References

[1] Ez. 38:11-13

[2] 1 Thes. 5:3

[3] Joel 2:28

[4] 1 Thes. 5:3

[5] Joel 2:30-31

[6] Rev. 7:1-8

[7] Dan. 9:27

[8] 2 Thes. 2:3-4

[9] Matt. 24:20

[10] Rev. 9:1-11

[11] Matt. 24:15-21

[12] Rev. 13:14-15

[13] Luke 21:20

[14] Matt. 24:15-20

[15] Rev. 9:6

[16] Rev. 9:10

[17] Matt. 24:9

[18] Dan. 11:44-45; Ez. 38-39; Rev. 16:12-14, 16

[19] Matt. 24:30

[20] Rom. 11:26

[21] Rev. 19:11-12

[22] Is. 63:1

[23] Zech. 14:4

[24] Zech. 14:5

[25] Zech. 14:12-13

[26] Rev. 16:16

[27] Rev. 19:20

[28] Rom. 11:26

CHAPTER 6

The Nations

Up until the very end, the nations will continue to behave as they currently do—with wars, rumors of wars, and conflict. As the end approaches, China will be expanding throughout Southeast Asia and the Pacific. Russia will be attempting to expand, especially toward the Middle East. The ten-nation empire of the Antichrist around the Mediterranean and centered in Rome will be expanding as well—toward Israel, toward the east, and toward the south.[1] The covenant between the Antichrist and Israel, and perhaps with other nations, will have opened the door for his expansion. The United States will be greatly weakened and even more divided than it is now. None of the nations will expect what is about to happen to the whole Earth.

Shock and Terror

And I saw when he opened the sixth seal, and there was a great earthquake; and the sun became black as sackcloth of hair, and the whole moon became as blood; and the stars of the heaven fell unto the earth, as a fig tree casteth her unripe figs when she is shaken of a great wind. And the heaven was removed as a scroll when it is rolled up; and every mountain and island were moved out of their places. (Rev. 6:12-14)

Abruptly, the events of the sixth seal will shake the globe. The earthquake that shocks the Earth at that time will be enormous, extraordinary, something never experienced in human history. It will be so great that every mountain will be moved out of its place. The events of the sixth seal will be a warning to mankind concerning what is about to come upon the Earth, and it will be a foretaste of what is about to occur.

Men, women, children, kings, paupers—men of every race, nation, and status—will hide underground, hoping to somehow survive what will shortly strike the Earth. The events of the seventh seal and the first four trumpets will then follow.

Devastation

And the first sounded, and there followed hail and fire, mingled with blood, and they were cast upon the earth: and the third part of the earth was burnt up, and the third part of the trees was burnt up, and all green grass was burnt up. And the second angel sounded, and as it were a great mountain burning with fire was cast into the sea: and the third part of the sea became blood; and there died the third part of the creatures which were in the sea, even they that had life; and the third part of the ships was destroyed. And the third angel sounded, and there fell from heaven a great star, burning as a torch, and it fell upon the third part of the rivers, and upon the fountains of the waters; and the name of the star is called Wormwood: and the third part of the waters became wormwood; and many men died of the waters, because they were made bitter. And the fourth angel sounded, and the third part of the sun was smitten, and the third part of the moon, and the third part of the stars; that the third part of them should be darkened, and the day should not shine for the third part of it, and the night in like manner. (Rev. 8:7-12)

Most of Asia will be burned by fire; the whole Earth will suffer enormous heat; a massive asteroid will strike the Pacific; then another large asteroid will strike the Himalayas. Gigantic tsunamis will demolish the Pacific Rim as well as much of the Atlantic coastline. A large portion of the Earth will be darkened by the debris and the ash from the numerous meteors passing through the Earth's atmosphere.

Much of the Earth will suffer great devastation. Southern Europe and the Middle East will be largely spared. However, the Pacific Rim will be obliterated. Asia will suffer great destruction, with fires and great heat scorching both it and the entire Earth. The areas around the Atlantic will also suffer much devastation.

The result of all these judgments will be the upending of the world we know. Throughout most of the Earth, there will be no electricity. *Consider this: there will be no electricity.* Virtually all communications will cease. Food supplies, as well as potable water, will be extremely scarce. It will be an unspeakably difficult time. People will struggle to survive.

Temperatures will first shoot upward from the enormous amount of energy released by the asteroids and meteors striking the Earth. Then, temperatures will plummet as the darkened atmosphere allows little sunlight through to warm the Earth. The frigid north will be nearly lifeless.

The End of the Nations

During this last three and a half years, war will continue in Asia;[2] the Antichrist will continue his expansion into North Africa;[3] Russia will be preparing to invade the Middle East;[4] the United States will become a wilderness.[5]

Very near the end of this age, three great armies will invade Israel. Russia will come down from the north over the mountains and into Israel.[6] Asian armies from the East will amass at the Euphrates.[7] That great river will be dried up, allowing these to also invade Israel.[8] The Antichrist will invade from Egypt.[9]

When they have gathered in Israel, before they initiate battle with each other, the Lord will appear in the heavens, followed by His armies.[10] The slaughter will be terrible as the Lord obliterates all those forces arrayed in Israel.[11] Not one of the invaders will remain.

The Nations
During the Endtime

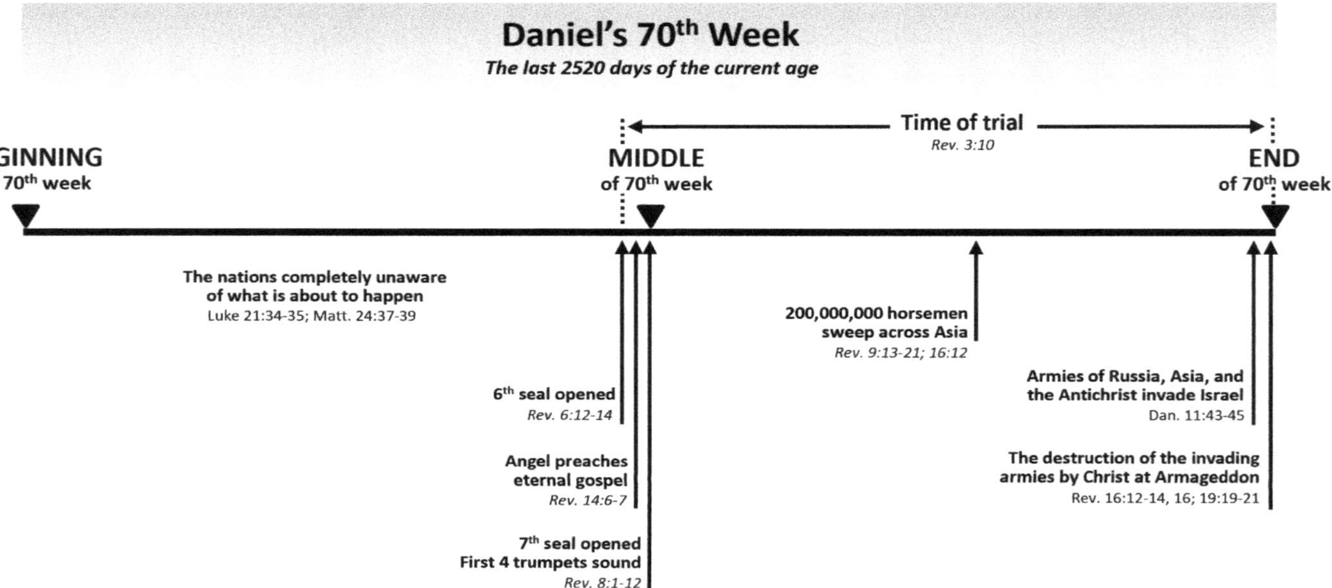

References

[1] Dan. 8:9
[2] Rev. 9:13-19; 16:12
[3] Dan. 11:42-43
[4] Ez. 38:10-12
[5] Rev. 12:6, 14
[6] Ez. 38:21-22; 39:4
[7] Rev. 16:12-14, 16
[8] Rev. 16:12
[9] Dan. 11:43-45
[10] Rev. 19:11-15
[11] Rev. 14:19-20

CHAPTER 7

The Antichrist

In addition to the nations, the Church, and Israel, there are other notable names playing a crucial role during the endtime. One of these is the Antichrist. He will arise from among the ten nations[1] that will eventually compose his empire. He will rise to power quickly, subduing those who oppose him.[2] Among other great abilities, he will be able to solve problems that previously seemed intractable.[3]

As the end approaches, something will happen in Israel that causes her to become open to an agreement into which she might not otherwise have entered. This will probably occur as a result of some serious existential crisis in Israel. Apparently, the Antichrist will provide Israel with security and certain other provisions in exchange for something vital to her. However, the Bible does not tell us what that is. This agreement will be for seven years.[4]

The First Three and a Half Years

During the first half of these last seven years, the Antichrist will be expanding toward the east, the south, and toward Israel.[5] No one will be able to stop him.[6] He will be enabled by Satan himself and, no doubt, by amazing technology. During these years, he will honor his pact with Israel.

The Last Three and a Half Years

Near the middle of the last seven years, the Antichrist will be slain by the sword.[7] Then, to the amazement of the whole world, he will come back to life.[8] He will cause the animal sacrifices at the Temple to cease,[9] and sit in the Jewish Temple, declaring himself to be God.[10] Through one of his allies, he will set up an idol of himself in the Temple.[11] This image will be able to speak and force Jews to worship it, under penalty of death.[12] Both the idol and the mark will likely exhibit advanced technology, such as artificial intelligence and cerebral implants.* The Antichrist will blaspheme God,[13] and wear out and overcome those saints[14] in Israel who will be telling of the Lord's imminent coming.

During the last three and a half years, the Antichrist will continue to expand his empire. As the end approaches, he will be in North Africa.[15] He will hear tidings from the east and north, as the armies of Asia and Russia begin advancing upon Israel.[16] He will return to Israel with great fury[17] to battle the invading hosts, and set up his camp near Armageddon.[18] Christ will then appear to deliver Israel from the invaders.[19] The battle will end at Armageddon.[20] There the Antichrist will be taken alive, and then cast into the lake of fire.[21] No one, including Satan, will be able to deliver him from that fate.[22]

---

* For a further explanation of the role of technology in the Antichrist's rise to power and conquests, see the book, *The Beast, His Image, and His Mark.*

The Antichrist
During the Endtime

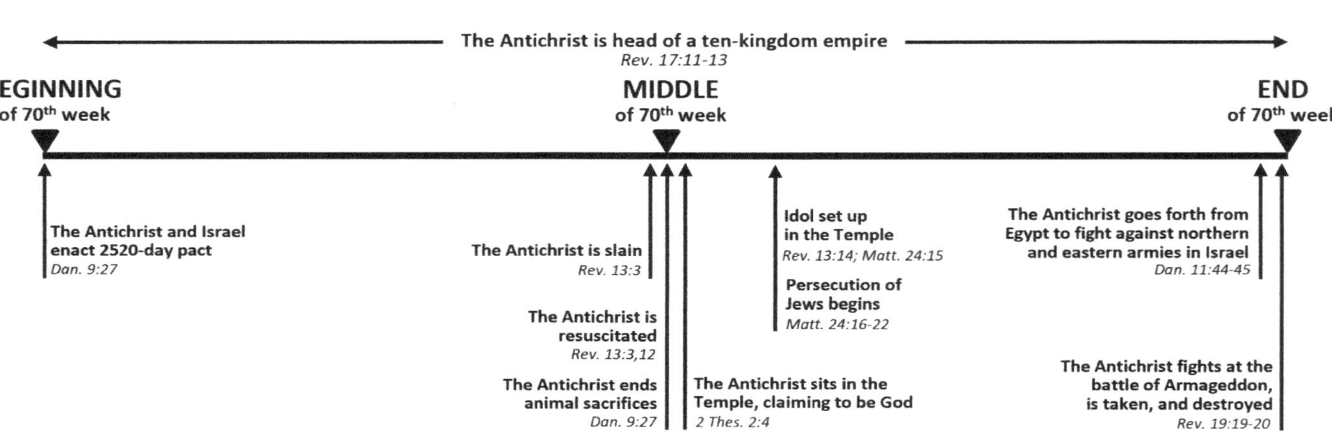

References

[1] Dan. 7:7-8, 24

[2] Dan. 7:8, 24

[3] Dan. 7:8

[4] Dan. 9:27

[5] Dan. 8:9

[6] Rev. 13:4

[7] Rev. 13:3, 14

[8] Rev. 13:14

[9] Dan. 9:27

[10] 2 Thes. 2:4

[11] Rev. 13:14-15

[12] Rev. 13:15

[13] Rev. 13:6

[14] Rev. 13:7; Dan. 7:21, 25; 12:7

[15] Dan. 11:42-43

[16] Dan. 11:44

[17] Dan. 11:44

[18] Dan. 11:45

[19] Rev. 19:11-13

[20] Rev. 16:16

[21] Rev. 19:19-20

[22] Dan. 11:45

CHAPTER 8

Ushering In the Kingdom

In the previous chapters, we have seen what takes place on the Earth during the last seven years of this age. The great, earthshaking events of that time will thoroughly and literally change the face of our planet. The mountains and islands will change.[1] The flora and fauna will change. Most importantly, humanity will change. Nothing will be the same again. A logical question to ask is, What happens then? What takes place immediately after the seven years of which we have spoken?

The Christians will have been judged at the judgment seat of Christ,[2] and received either a reward or a punishment,[3] based upon how they have behaved and what they have done in their Christian life. However, Christ will not have finished His dealings with the two other peoples on Earth—the Jews and the nations.

Gathering Israel and the Nations

And he shall send forth his angels with a great sound of a trumpet, and they shall gather together his elect from the four winds, from one end of heaven to the other. (Matt. 24:31)

The first thing Christ will do upon His return is to send out His angels with the great sound of a trumpet to gather all of His elect—all the Jews remaining on Earth—back to Israel. The Jews will be scattered throughout the nations during the last years of this age.[4] Many will be in exile, imprisoned, or enslaved. All of these must be gathered to Israel to stand before the Lord.

In addition, all the people of the nations who remain alive will also be gathered to Israel, specifically to the valley of Jehoshaphat.[5] There, they will await the Lord's judgment upon them. Finally, the angels will gather everything that offends from throughout the Earth to cleanse the Earth of all the evil one's works.[6]

It will take ten days to gather all the living to Israel.* The nations will escort the Jews back, knowing they are both the Lord's brothers and His chosen people. They will treat the Jews with utmost respect, recognizing that God is with them. They will bring the Jews back on horses and camels, in carriages, and any other way possible.[7]

How it will be possible to return all the Jews, as well as all the peoples of the nations, to Israel in a mere ten days, without our current means of transportation, is unknown. The angels will gather humanity from the four corners of the Earth, and all that remain will come to Israel. Although we don't know how that is possible, the angels will have a way.

Face-to-face

As I live, saith the Lord Jehovah, surely with a mighty hand, and with an outstretched arm, and with wrath poured out, will I be king over you: and I will bring you out from the peoples, and will gather you out of the countries wherein ye are scattered, with a mighty hand, and with an outstretched arm, and with wrath poured out . . . (Ez. 20:33-34)

By the tenth day† after the Lord's return, all the Jews will be in Israel. Christ will then address them face-to-face,[8] and enter into judgment with them. He will shine upon their unbelief and upon the hatred they once held toward Him. The Lord will show them His death for them. He will let them see the depth of their corruption.

---

* In the Old Testament there were seven feasts, four of which have been fulfilled. The Feasts of Passover and Unleavened Bread were fulfilled at the time of the Lord's death. The Feast of Firstfruits was fulfilled on the day of the Lord's resurrection. The Feast of Weeks was fulfilled on the day of Pentecost. There are still three feasts remaining unfulfilled. Their fulfillment will occur at the time of the Lord's return. At His return He will send forth His angels with the sound of a great trumpet, to gather the Jews back to Israel—this will be the true Feast of Trumpets. This feast lasts ten days during which the Jews will be gathered back to Israel.

† On the tenth day will be the true Day of Atonement. The Jews will see Christ's atonement for them, and weep and mourn until the fifteenth day.

When the Jews see what they have done, how they have behaved, and perceived the secrets of their own hearts, they will weep and mourn bitterly.[9] All the families will mourn separately, and the wives will mourn apart from their families.[10] This may be because the women will take the lead to oppose Christ.

The mourning in Israel will last for five days.* It is doubtful that any of the Jews will be able to eat during that time. This will be the genuine fast.

At the end of those days, the Jews' mourning will be over. They will then enter into Christ's earthly kingdom, and enjoy genuine peace and security for the first time. Nothing will be able to harm them again.

Judgment

But when the Son of man shall come in his glory, and all the angels with him, then shall he sit on the throne of his glory: and before him shall be gathered all the nations: and he shall separate them one from another, as the shepherd separateth the sheep from the goats; and he shall set the sheep on his right hand, but the goats on the left. (Matt. 24:31-33)

All the Lord's brothers will accompany Him to the valley of Jehoshaphat, where the Gentiles will be waiting. The angels[11] will separate the people, one from another. They will place the "sheep" at the Lord's right hand, and the "goats" at His left.

Sitting upon the throne of His glory, The Lord will tell the ones at His right to enter into the kingdom prepared for them from the foundation of the world.[12] They will be the blessed of the Lord's Father. He will tell them that when He was hungry, they fed Him; when He was thirsty, they gave Him drink; when He was a stranger, naked, sick, or in prison, they ministered to Him. They will ask Him when they had ever done such things. He will say in that they did it to one of the least of His brothers, they did it to Him. Looking upon the Lord's many brothers, they will see the one or ones they had helped during the endtime. These blessed of the nations will then enter into eternal life.[13]

---

* That is, until the true Feast of Tabernacles.

The Lord will then turn to the goats on His left, and tell them to depart from Him into the eternal fire prepared for the devil and his angels, for they are accursed.[14] When He was hungry, they did not feed Him; when He was thirsty, they gave Him no drink; when he was naked, sick, or in prison, they did not minister to Him. They will ask the Lord when they ever did such things to Him. He will respond in that they did it to one of the least of His brothers, they did it to Him. Looking upon the Lord's many brothers, they will see the one or ones they mistreated during the endtime. They will depart into the eternal fire. I do not doubt this will cause great sadness to the Lord—He does not want any to perish.[15]

Establishing the Kingdom

The nations will be cared for by those believers who have received the authority to rule from the Lord.[16] In Israel, the Lord will cleanse the temple of all the defilement to which it had been subjected. This will take another 15 days.[17] The Lord will then institute the earthly priesthood of the Jews. This will take yet another 45 days.[18]

Recovering the Earth

The Earth will be in a complete shambles. For some time the Jews, and probably all the nations as well, will dwell in makeshift enclosures.* Slowly, over time, they will proceed to change both their dwellings and the Earth around them, to gradually enter into the millennial state.

The whole Earth will become a place of immense beauty—an enlarged garden of Eden. It will shine with the Lord's glory and the glory of God's many sons like a brilliant, universal diamond. It is such a state that will usher in the new heaven and new Earth with the New Jerusalem.

---

* That is, in tabernacles, as the Feast of Tabernacles foreshadowed.

References

[1] Rev. 16:17-21

[2] 2 Cor. 5:10

[3] Matt. 25:14-30

[4] Zech. 14:2; Joel 3:2-3

[5] Joel 3:1-2, 12

[6] Matt. 13:41

[7] Is. 66:20

[8] Ez. 20:34-35

[9] Zech. 12:10-11

[10] Zech. 12:12-13

[11] Matt. 13:47-50

[12] Matt. 25:34

[13] Matt. 25:46

[14] Matt. 25:41

[15] 1 Tim. 2:3-4

[16] Luke 19:16-19

[17] Dan. 12:11

[18] Dan. 12:12

CHAPTER 9

Conclusion

From the picture painted in the preceding chapters, it should be clear that the middle of the last seven years will be traumatic, dramatic, and tumultuous. Many grave things occur in a very brief period of time: the church age closes and the testimony of Jesus passes from the Church to the sealed of Israel;[1] the Antichrist is slain and then brought back to life by the spirit of another from the abyss,[2] changing his character into the utterly malicious being he is during the last three and a half years of the age; the current world, as we now experience it, ends in the fire of numerous asteroid strikes.[3]

That point in time is a kind of nexus, in which God has brought together many "threads" and intervened to deal with them all at the same time. This is something only God could do! We must be aware of what is about to come upon the Earth, and prepare accordingly.

In addition, as we look for the signs of the end, we must not neglect our current Christian life. We must spend our time in prayer, in fellowship, and in pouring out to others what God has given us. Above all, we must cultivate an intimate relationship with the Lord, followed closely by genuine love for the brethren. Through these, we will mature into what the Lord desires, and it is this maturity in life in the believers that will, in fact, bring the Lord back.

The timing of all things—including the signs of His return—are in the Lord's hands. He can move quickly to accomplish them. What is not easy for the Lord is to gain us—to gain our hearts and minds. For this, He needs our day-by-day cooperation, allowing Him to do all that is in His heart within us. Giving the Lord such a free way allows Him to move quickly on the Earth for His return.

Be wise, brothers and sisters! Let us use our time wisely. Let us follow the example of our dear brother, the apostle Paul, who counted all things as refuse that he might gain Christ. If we are honest with the Lord, we will acknowledge that we still have too little Christ within us. Let us pursue Him, following Him into the eternal state God has prepared for us.

References

[1] Rev. 7:2-8; 12:17
[2] Rev. 9:11; 11:7; 17:8
[3] Rev. 8:5-12

BIBLIOGRAPHY

Cozza, Paul. *The Coming End of the Age.*
A Place in the Wilderness, 2016

———————— *The Beast, His Image, and His Mark.*
A Place in the Wilderness, 2018

———————— *Firstfruits and Harvest.*
A Place in the Wilderness, 2019

———————— *Greapa.*
Wipf & Stock, 2023